© 2001 by Barbour Publishing, Inc.

ISBN 1-58660-255-1

Cover art © Photo Disc

All Scripture quotations, unless otherwise noted, are from the HOLY BIBLE, NEW INTERNATIONAL VERSION® NIV®. Copyright 1973, 1978, 1984 by International Bible Society. Used by permission of Zondervan Publishing House. All rights reserved.

Scripture quotations marked KJV are from the King James Version of the Bible.

Published by Barbour Books, an imprint of Barbour Publishing, Inc., P.O. Box 719, Uhrichsville, Ohio 44683 www.barbourbooks.com

Member of the
Evangelical Christian
Publishers Association

Printed in China.
5 4 3

Good Tidings of Great Joy

Ellyn Sanna

DayMaker
GREETING BOOKS

AND, lo, the angel of the Lord came upon them,
and the glory of the Lord shone round about them:
and they were sore afraid.

And the angel said unto them,
Fear not: for, behold,
I bring you good tidings of great joy,
which shall be to all people.

LUKE 2:9–10 KJV

CONTENTS

MOST of us have waited with dread and anticipation for the results of some important exam or medical test. We feared the worst. And then at last. . .good news! What a sense of relief and joy swept through us when we heard that we no longer had anything to fear.

If we really understood the meaning of Christmas, we would feel that same joyful relief. Christmas is the best news ever: Jesus Christ, the Son of God, came to earth to live with us. And because He came, nothing will ever be the same. The glad tidings of Christmas tell us that the world is made new in Jesus. . .our very selves are made new. . .and through Jesus, a new eternal day has dawned for us all. Because of Him, we will never die.

Can you imagine any better tidings than that? After all, that is what "gospel" really means—*good news*.

A NEW WORLD

He who was seated on the throne said,
"I am making everything new!"

REVELATION 21:5

WE all know the way things work in the world:

"Me first."
"Survival of the fittest."
"The rich get richer,
and the poor get poorer."

But at Christmas, Jesus brought us good news: In the Kingdom of God, things are different. The King Himself laid down His life to become small and poor and humble. Christmas creates an entirely new world, a world where everything is turned backward and upside down.

YOU know that that those who are regarded
as rulers of the Gentiles
lord it over them, and their high officials exercise authority
over them. Not so with you. Instead,
whoever wants to become great among you
must be your servant, and whoever wants
to be first must be slave of all.
For even the Son of Man did not come be served,
but to serve, and to give his life as a ransom for many."

MARK 10:42–45

*And a little child
will lead them.*

ISAIAH 11:6

THE day and the spirit of Christmas rearrange the world parade. As the world arranges it, usually there come first in importance—leading the parade with a big blare of a band—the Big Shots. . . . Then at the tail end, as of little importance, trudge the weary, the poor, the lame, the halt, and the blind. But in the Christmas spirit, the procession is turned around. Those at the tail end are put first in the arrangement of the Child of Christmas.

HALFORD E. LUCCOCK

WHEN compassion for the common man was born on Christmas Day, with it was born new hope among the multitudes. They feel a great, ever-rising determination to lift themselves and their children out of hunger and disease and misery, up to a higher level. Jesus started a fire upon the earth, and it is burning hot today, the fire of a new hope in the hearts of the hungry multitudes.

FRANK C. LAUBACH

*How can we claim to have. . .
"good news" unless people can see in us that Jesus Christ is
breaking down barriers and bringing us together?*

ALBERT BRAITHWAITE

*"Glory to God in the highest,
and on earth peace to men
on whom his favor rests."*

LUKE 2:14

*Jesus' good news, then,
was that the Kingdom of God had come,
and that He, Jesus, was its herald and expounder to men.
More than that, in some special and mysterious way,
He was the kingdom.*

MALCOLM MUGGERIDGE

WELCOME! *all Wonders in one sight!*
Eternity shut in a span.
Summer in winter, day in night,
Heaven in earth, and God in man.
Great little One! Whose all-embracing birth
Lifts earth to heaven, stoops heav'n to earth!

RICHARD CRASHAW

*Sometimes we can hardly believe the glad news
that Christmas offers our hearts. . . .*

WHY do we not know the country whose citizens we are? Because we have wandered so far away that we have forgotten it. But the Lord Christ, the king of that land, came down to us and drove forgetfulness from our hearts. God took to Himself our flesh so that He might be our way back.

AUGUSTINE

THE trouble is this—that the range of our thinking is now so blinkered, so little and small, that we cannot see the high, wonderful wisdom and the power and goodness of the blessed Trinity. And this is what He means when He says: "You shall see for yourself that all manner of things shall be well." It was as if He said: "Have faith, and have trust, and at the last day you shall see it all transformed into great joy."

JULIAN OF NORWICH

NO *more let sins and sorrows grow,*
Nor thorns infest the ground;
He comes to make His blessings flow
Far as the curse is found.

He rules the world with truth and grace,
And makes the nations prove
The glories of His righteousness,
And wonders of His love.

ISAAC WATTS

DESPITE the good tidings that Christmas brings, people continue to shut their hearts to Jesus, the message God sent to us from heaven. Because we turn away from Jesus, evil continues to exist on earth.

But if we throw our hearts wide open to that same glad news the angels brought to the shepherds so long ago, then our hearts will become little Bethlehems. Jesus will be born anew in us, and through us His kingdom will be visible on earth.

Our world may seem old and dingy—but Jesus makes all things new and clean.

A NEW WAY TO LIVE

"A new command I give you:
Love one another.
As I have loved you,
so you must love one another."

JOHN 13:34

MORE than two thousand years ago, the angels brought their glad tidings to a bunch of shepherds who were huddled with their sheep on a cold hillside. *The Son of God is born!* the angels sang on that long-ago dark night.

On the darkest, coldest nights this world offers, Jesus can be birthed anew in our own hearts—and in Him we will find an entirely new way to live. No longer will we put ourselves at the center of the world; no longer will we push and shove to get what we want. Instead, we will follow a new path—the path of love.

WHAT are we to make of Jesus Christ? . . .
The real question is not what are we to make of Christ,
but what is He to make of us?

C. S. LEWIS

JESUS points to the possibility of a life without worries,
a life in which all things are made new.

HENRY NOUWEN

Where there is love, there is Jesus.

MADELEINE L'ENGLE

O *little town of Bethlehem*
How still we see thee lie!
Above thy deep and dreamless sleep
The silent stars go by.
Yet in thy dark streets shineth
The everlasting Light;
The hopes and fears of all the years
Are met in thee tonight.

How silently, how silently,
The wondrous gift is giv'n!
So God imparts to human hearts
The blessings of His Heav'n.
No ear may hear His coming,
But in this world of sin,
Where meek souls will receive Him still,
The dear Christ enters in.

PHILLIPS BROOKS

OUR lives are destined to
become like the life of Jesus.
The whole purpose of Jesus' ministry is
to bring us to the house of the Father.
Not only did Jesus come to free us from
the bonds of sin and death,
He also came to lead us into the
intimacy of His divine life.

HENRY NOUWEN

INCREASINGLY I rejoiced in the gospel—the amazing good news—that the Creator of what to us human beings is this bewildering and unimaginably vast universe, so loved the world that He gave His only Son, that whosoever believes in Him should not perish, but have everlasting life. Everlasting life, I came to see, is not just continued existence but a growing knowledge— not merely intellectual but wondering through trust, love, and fellowship—of Him who alone is truly God, and Jesus Christ whom He has sent.

KENNETH SCOTT LATOURETTE

ACCORDING to the old world's way of looking at things, all of us are condemned to die sooner or later. But like a prisoner on death row who receives a last-minute pardon, we, too, have escaped the sentence of death. We have been rescued. . .redeemed. . .and we are now the children of God who will live forever in the life of His Son.

But when the time had fully come, God sent his Son,
born of a woman, born under law,
to redeem those under law,
that we might receive the full rights of sons.

GALATIANS 4:4–5

[H]istory. . .centered on the Messiah
who came on a rescue mission,
who died and who wrought from that death
the salvation of the world.

PHILIP YANCEY

Never offer men
a thimbleful of gospel.
The gospel offers a man life. . .
a life abundant in love.

HENRY DRUMMOND

The Christ Himself, the Son of God who is man (just like you) and God (just like His Father) is actually at your side. . . . He is beginning to turn you into the same kind of thing as Himself. He is beginning, so to speak, to "inject" His kind of life and thought. . .into you.

C. S. LEWIS

LISTEN to the angel's song, all you who have a troubled heart. "I bring you good tidings of great joy!" Never let the thought cross your mind that Christ is angry with you! He did not come to condemn you. If you want to define Christ rightly, then pay heed to how the angel defines Him: namely, "A great joy!"

MARTIN LUTHER

He does not force our wills
but only takes what we give Him,
but He does not give Himself entirely until
He sees that we yield ourselves entirely to Him.

TERESA OF AVILA

OH, thank You, Jesus, for being born for us,
and living for us, and dying for us, and rising for us,
and sending us the Holy Spirit.
Thank You, with thanks beyond words,
but must be expressed in the lovingness of our lives.

MADELEINE L'ENGLE

A NEW DAY

See, darkness covers the earth
and thick darkness is over the peoples,
but the LORD rises upon you
and His glory appears over you.
Arise, shine, for your light has come,
and the glory of the LORD rises upon you.

ISAIAH 60:2, 1

Sunrise at the far horizon was
sunrise near me in this infant.

WALTER WANGERIN, JR.

SOMETIMES life seems like a long dark night that will never end. Troubles pile on top of troubles; heartaches are everywhere we turn. And in the end we die.

What a bleak outlook! But the good tidings of Christmas mean that a new day has dawned, an eternal day. Like children who wake up after a nightmare, we can leap into this new day with joy and relief. Because of Jesus, we need never fear death again.

Long is our winter; Dark is our night;
Come, set us free, O Saving Light!

FIFTEENTH-CENTURY GERMAN HYMN

HIGH o'er the lonely hills black turns to gray,
Bird-song the valley fills, mists fold away;
Gray wakes to green again,
Beauty is seen again,
Gold and serene again dawneth the day.

So, o'er the hills of life, stormy, forlorn,
Out of the cloud and strife sunrise is born;
Swift grows the light for us,
Ended is night for us,
Soundless and bright for us breaketh God's morn.

Bid then farewell to sleep: rise up and run!
What though the hill be steep? Strength's in the sun.
Now you shall find at last
Night's left behind at last,
And for mankind at last, day has begun!

JAN STRUTHER

CANDLES are always popular for giving a warm romantic glow. . . . Of course a candle is easy to blow out! . . . But there are also the special party candles that keep bursting back into life. They are a much better picture of the light of the gospel! For though there have been numerous attempts down the centuries to extinguish the light, it has kept on bursting back into flame.

The light of Christ keeps on shining.

DAVID BONNERT

AWAY *in a manger,*
No crib for a bed,
The little Lord Jesus,
Laid down His sweet head.
The stars in the sky,
Looked down where He lay,
The little Lord Jesus,
Asleep on the hay.

Be near me, Lord Jesus,
I ask Thee to stay
Close by me forever,
And love me, I pray;
Bless all the dear children
In thy tender care,
And fit us for heaven
To live with Thee there.

ANONYMOUS

31

Exactly as though it were morning and not the night,
the shepherds went out into the city and began immediately
to tell everyone
what the angel had said about this child.
They left a trail of startled people behind them,
as on they went, both glorifying and praising God.

WALTER WANGERIN, JR.

LIKE the shepherds who heard the angels' wonderful tidings, we, too, can forget the night we see around us. We know the day has dawned.

If you commit yourself to this belief, those around you may be as startled and disbelieving at those who heard the shepherds' news. But why walk in the darkness anymore when the Christmas star shines bright as day?

OUR Savior, the Dayspring from on high,
has visited us,
And we who were in darkness
and shadows have found the truth!

BYZANTINE PRAYER

AND we have the word of
the prophets made more certain,
and you will do well to pay attention to it,
as to a light shining in a dark place,
until the day dawns and the morning star
rises in your hearts.

2 PETER 1:19

The people living in darkness
have seen a great light.

MATTHEW 4:16

God appears and God is light
To those poor souls who dwell in night.

WILLIAM BLAKE

For God, who said, "Let light shine out of darkness,"
made his light shine in our hearts
to give us the light of the knowledge
of the glory of God in the face of Christ.

2 CORINTHIANS 4:6

In darkness there is no choice.
It is light that enables us to see
the differences between things:
and it is Christ who gives us light.

C. T. WHITMELL

IN the darkness of night we wander around confused, anxious, lost. We do not know which way to go; we cannot choose what would be best for our lives. But at Christmas, God sent us tidings of great joy—a new day has dawned, and by the light of Jesus we now can see.

Lord Jesus Christ,
. . .You are the radiant star of morning.
Come and deliver us from our fears
And the darkness in our everyday lives.

VICTOR-ANTOINE D'AVILA-LATOURRETTE

DAWN is a gift given to us that we might see in it the face of God. It is a time to acknowledge His presence and power in the glory of His creation. It is a time to revel in the pageantry and color of creation. At dawn God opens His hand; glory shines forth, and eternal light dispels night.

ELDYN SIMONS

BUT the path of the just is as the shining light, that shineth more and more unto the perfect day.

PROVERBS 4:18 KJV

The people walking in darkness
have seen a great light;
on those living in the land of
the shadow of death a light has dawned.

ISAIAH 9:2

For he that is mighty
hath done to me great things.

LUKE 1:49 KJV

The great thing, and the only thing,
is to adore and praise God.

THOMAS MERTON

O come, all ye faithful, joyful and triumphant,
O come ye, O come ye, to Bethlehem;
Come and behold Him, born the King of angels.
O come, let us adore Him, Christ the Lord.

Yea, Lord, we greet Thee, born this happy morning;
Jesus, to Thee be glory given.
Word of the Father, now in flesh appearing.
O come, let us adore Him, Christ the Lord.

JOHN FRANCIS WADE

AN angel of the Lord appeared to him in a dream and said, "Joseph son of David, do not be afraid to take Mary home as your wife, because what is conceived in her is from the Holy Spirit. She will give birth to a son, and you are to give him the name Jesus, because he will save his people from their sins." All this took place to fulfill what the Lord had said through the prophet: "The virgin will be with child and will give birth to a son, and they will call him Immanuel"—which means, "God with us."

MATTHEW 1:20–23

Sometimes the glad tidings of Christmas
seem simply too good to be true. But. . .

As you keep quiet and listen, you will know,
deep down in your heart,
that you are loved. As the air is around about you,
so is His love around about you. Trust that love. . . .
It will never ever fail.

AMY CARMICHAEL